I0159418

Who does God say *you are?*

By: Caleb Anderson, Min.

God's Place Publishing

GOD'S PLACE PUBLISHING

First Edition
Printed in the United States
WHO DOES GOD SAY YOU ARE?
Copyright © 2013 by God's Place Inc.
Cover design © Caleb Anderson
The Place Logo © God's Place Inc. 2012
Cover Pictures provided by Dream Times, Inc.
ISBN-13: 978-0615930404
ISBN-10: 0615930409

All rights reserved.

No part of this book may be reproduced, scanned,
or distributed in any printed or electronic form
without permission. Please do not participate in or
encourage piracy of copyright materials in viola-
tion of the author's rights.

Purchase only authorized editions.

Forward

"Every good and perfect gift is from above, coming down from the Father of the heavenly lights, who does not change like shifting shadows" (James 1:17).

It is my hope that this will actually be the first of three books on the Gifts of God. This is not about our natural talents and abilities. Although we may use those abilities to God's glory, they can also operate apart from the power of his Holy Spirit. The Gifts of God can only function in the spiritual realm and have a different source and power than our 'natural' abilities.

As the first of the three hoped-for books, this one explores the gifts of character Father has given to ALL people and listed in Romans 12:3-8. Character gifts determine the core values of our inmost being. As Christians we all love Truth since that is Jesus himself. However, a person with the character and core values of a prophet will typically see all situations in terms of God's black and white Truth. A person with the character and core values of mercy will typically see all situations in terms of God's grace and mercy for a person's need. Which is correct? Of course, each thinks their own perception is correct since it is essentially filtered through the core values of their particular character giftedness. In the reality of our messy lives, we are also quite often a mixture of two or more of these gifts. Each of the seven character gifts is part of the identity of Jesus who is the perfection and completion of all seven.

Perhaps the greatest danger in studying the gifts is that we typically become very self-focused. The study of the Spiritual Gifts should never be focused on self but on how each gift works together for the Body of Christ, i.e. the Church. Understanding our own character gifts and our own calling gifts can certainly help us grow as we study the value each one brings to the Body. However, it is far more important for me to understand and value the other character and calling gifts even more than my own. Remember the caution at the beginning of the Romans 12 passage: "Do not think of yourself more highly than you ought."

Refusing to use the spiritual gifts God has given us not only robs him of his glory, but also prevents others in the Body from growing into the spiritual maturity of Christ Jesus. No matter how much we may develop our own spiritual gifts, we are not capable of reaching maturity without the entire Body functioning in each of its separate giftings. Obviously, no gift has sufficient value or significance by itself. Each gift is of greatest value when it is appropriately fitted together with all of the other parts of the Body. Only then does the "whole body . . . grow and build itself up in love, as each part does its work."

Caleb has approached this work as an artist and an art critic. Taking each gift as one would a master painting. I can easily assure you that there is not another book on spiritual gifts anything like this delightful work. I have had the pleasure of working with this material which was first developed by a pastor friend who was an interesting complex of both exhorter and teacher. I have taught this material with my own character/calling biases. And now I can see through Caleb's filters of his prophetic/teacher giftings with a special seasoning of God's creative character in this writer/artist.

More than 'learning to understand' these seven character gifts, I hope you simply receive the revelation of the Holy Spirit as He unfolds the 'seven spirits of God.' Have fun! Discover who God says you are by His creative design and find your own place in His household, the Church.

Don Youts

Questions

(Who am I?)

It was a warm summer day. The freshly remodeled lounge reeked of classical maleness. And that was the point. The local Christian pregnancy center was taking a radical new approach to the issue of unplanned births, unwanted children, and abortion. They wanted to engage, not just the crying women who revolved through their doors, but the dads too. The theory was simple: get the dads on board, and the women will be more likely to feel secure, supported... to feel OK about it all. I was one of the first guinea pigs- eager to be experimented on. Just another young Christian man who wanted to help. Just wanted to make a difference.

My teacher looked me over and, after the obligatory small talk, asked me a question I had never heard nor considered in my life. "Who does God say you are?" I was taken aback by the frankness of the statement. For it implies a level of personal attention from God I never considered myself worthy of. For in that simple question, a rush of little spoken of consequences bubble to the surface. Not least of which was that I had no clue how to answer.

For in considering what the Almighty thought individually of me, I would have to deal with the disturbing notion **God is really real**. Sure, I believed in God, I had been 'saved' a year before, after all. I learned a lot about God and saw the logic in a single creator of all this wondrous order. But in that question, God slipped from the mantel of religious icon and fell into my very present world. Suddenly the idea of God having opinions, and opinions about me no less, was terrifying. And what was equally terrifying was the knowledge that I hadn't a clue what the answer was. I had dedicated my life to a being without knowing what He thought of me, what He had to say about me, or who He called me.

I knew who I said I was. I had developed that through years of watching T.V. and movies like most other American kids of the last century. I knew who my parents thought I was. My father had made his academic visions for me clear even from a young age. "Of my sons," he would say, "you could get a Ph.D." And sure, I was even comfortable with what the bible had to say generally about mankind. We are all sinners (Romans 3:23). We are lost without Christ (John 14:6). He makes us whole again and we should be like Christ (Ephesians 5:1-2). But the idea of God, Father God, having a name for me- just me. That He has an opinion of me, well...

that was more than I could bear.

I found the verses about God's plans and destinies much more personal after that. Gone were the clichés of "God has a plan." They were replaced with, "What if I am God's plan?" And that was the most horrifying thought of all. For suddenly I felt the weight of God's authority given to Adam (Genesis 1:26) come firmly on my shoulders. The burden lay on my chest. And the sting of Christ's command to do what He did enter my veins (John 14:12).

For if God has personal opinions about me, I join the ranks of biblical characters, do I not? God only gives names to bible men, like Jacob and Abraham. He only had opinions about kings and high priests. He doesn't do that for us, now. That was then. He was part of Abraham's family. He dined at Abraham's table, not mine.

But maybe He should.

Didn't Christ die so He could? Wasn't that what all those Easter messages I heard over the years said? So why doesn't He?

Oh how we have lost such an insane idea as God- family member. A real being, living with me, in my mess, in my life and not outside it. The disciples didn't ask Christ to teach them to pray so they could do miracles; Christ gave them the authority to do so with just His name. No, they asked Him that because of the long nights by the side of the road when they heard a man not praying to God, but talking to His dad. Never had such ease and casualness been used towards the Lord, and they wanted that. They wanted to eat with God; they wanted to be close to him. They wanted to know what God's thoughts were about them.

So who does God say you are?

He says you are a reflection of Him (2 Corinthians 3:18). Made in His image. Made in His likeness. He says you are wonderful (Psalm 139:14). But we miss what these things mean. I am wonderful because I am in the image of God. When we strip all that is not of God from me I am left with what He put there, and what He put there is aspects of Himself. We each have a bit of God's nature in us, which is why we have church, you know. So when all the parts are put together we see the whole.

So when I ask, Who does God say you are? I am really asking, What aspect of God are you hiding?

Passion

(The Prophet)

We all know him. He is the awkward kid of the awkward kids. Never able to say the right thing or do anything socially normal. His foot seems to take permanent residence in his mouth. His parents don't know what to do with him. His teachers don't understand him and his few friends mostly just laugh at his oddity.

It isn't that he is trying to be strange. We know the difference between the truly different and the want- to-be who wear their nerdism like a badge of honor. Always trying to offend or annoy. Always proclaiming how boring and

sad 'normal' people are. No, this one is different. He comes to his strangeness quite naturally. No tricks needed here. No wish to promote
it, just unable to hide it. He tries; he really does,
to fit in. He tries to come off as normal.

He listens carefully to what people say. How
they talk. What jokes work and which don't.
Then he tries to mimic what he has learned
and tends to be terrible at it. And even the few
that, through years of practice, get to a point of
hiding well in a crowd still feel off. They still
feel different. And everyone, including them,
knows it.

It is not an off-ness one can easily describe.
It is just there, glaring at every social interac-
tion. Like a giant elephant in the room everyone can feel but none can name. And it is the
worst kind of impolite- the accidental faux pas.
He is sincere in his offensiveness, ignorant in
his rudeness, and loving in his clingy habits.

It's not that he is hateful- he just doesn't get it. And we don't get him.

But imagine, if you will, that the spiritual is more than a word used to describe warm, fuzzy experiences at church camp. What if the spiritual is a raw, real, chaotic thing? What if it, like radiation, fills our space, affects us deeply, and yet remains unseen.

What if demons have names?

For if demons have names, then they have individuality. And if they are individuals, then they have personality. And if they are individuals with personality, then they really exist. And if demons really exist, this world, and how we see the unseen, changes completely.

Suddenly I must question if my porn problem is deeper than a self-control issue. Maybe my desire to cut my own arms until the blood runs red lacks a scientific cause. Maybe my father's temper and my mother's shame are much deeper than financial woes and a bad economy. And maybe, just maybe, God knew most of us would not know what to do about it.

So he formed some people in the aspect of himself that could see where we dare not. For that is what the word prophet means- seer or see- er. They see what we can't. What we won't. They aren't afraid of the dark because it is filled with the unknown like a child or timid woman. No, they are scared because they know exactly what lives there. They see because they must. They can't not see the evil, the lies, and the corruption of this world. They must see because God placed in them His passion for righteousness, for justice, and for truth. And when you are designed by the Almighty to see what is good, you naturally notice what is evil.

Without effort, the stench of corruption fills their nostrils. Without trying, they see through the lies and to the truth of things. They physically see the very real demon literally whispering in your ear. Literally placing his hand on your shoulder as you spit out one more white lie to save face. They may not understand what they see, but they see it all the same.

It makes social events awkward. These lovable weirdos don't see a nice get-together. They see through it. They see through us. They see the filth that is our hypocrisy. And the thicker we apply our mask of decency the quicker they see through it. They see our smile for what it is- fake. Our social niceties smell of lies, and they can't help but want to vomit. They know you hate your spouse. They know you refuse to submit to him even though the scripture say so.

But hey, it's the twenty first century, right?

So I talk bad about my pastor behind his back. But is that really that bad? He is wrong after all.

Now they probably can't form the words to reveal our sins but they know them all the same. And what is worse is we know they know them. Somewhere in us, we feel naked in front of their blank gaze. And the harder we try to hide, the more naked we feel.

So what do we do?

Lock them up.

He hears voices anyway. Sue- what's her face- said so. He has even been to the crazy house a few times already, heavens me. Plus, I am not sure he is a good person, let alone a good Christian. Always so blunt and brash. No social decency. In Sunday school last week he actually said he believed he could move moun-

tains. I guess he was referring to that verse in Matthew where Christ said we could, but please- that is just crazy talk. Anyway, he gives me the creeps. Must be a bad guy. Must not be normal or good.

And why wouldn't a prophet make us quiver in our seats? They hear from God.

Oh wait, God turned off the loud speaker a few thousand years ago. So sorry, guess there are no more prophets. That was for then, anyhow. Now we just have schizos.

So lock them up. Use chemicals to lobotomize them. Oh, you thought those drugs were supposed to help? Were supposed to cure him? No my dear, they just mellow him out. Make him easier to deal with. Lessen the screaming fits. It's the best way. What else can we do? Believe him when he says he sees monsters? Oh please, it is just a twist of the brain. A sickness

of the nerves. There really is no other explana-
tion. Plus we can't have people formed in God's
passion for righteousness running around, now
can we? They might make us uncomfortable.

So an entire aspect of God's nature rests
hidden in our mad houses. Imprisoned for seeing, hearing, and feeling what we can't accept
to be real. We are all too smart for such non-
sense anyway. Sure the bible says, but we are
modern people. Free of such superstitions. We
have more scholars, sciences, and knowledge
than any people before us. God doesn't need to
send prophets anymore. We have it all worked
out.

Or do we?

Without the prophet the church becomes
the world's whore, used as they please. With
no word of God, no passion of God, no fire of
God, we might as well become a social club

and go golfing instead of going to church. The prophet is the one who slaps us right in our complacency. He doesn't show us the light, he grabs us by the jaw and shoves our face into it. Then he thrusts us back into the shadows and yells in our ear, "See the difference yet? Do you see the difference yet?"

Feel violated?

Good, they want you to. They want to violate your casual existence just like the spirit world regularly violates theirs. They want you to feel the fire. Know the pressure. They want you to be pierced so deeply you can't help but bleed. Then when your guts are spilled out on the floor you might, you just might, get it. What do you get? You get that for years it hasn't been them that have failed to get it.

It has been you.

Certainly not the cheery Easter message we are so used to. But that is God's point. That is what he wants us to see in the prophet. "I'm not all sugar," He says. "Stop trying to make me nicer. I'm not a precious moment. I am also a fiery sword. And though I love my garden, I will cut whole branches off without a second thought."

The prophet is Romans 11:21 made flesh: "For if God did not spare the natural branches, He may not spare you either." They are His warning. If God wouldn't spare the Jews, what makes us think he will spare the Christians?

But these things are the unseen. And we wrestle with them terribly. So when the prophet, full of the spirit, yells, "Do you see?" the wise man will reply humbly, "No, I truly do not. Please teach me to set my eyes on the unseen."

Loving Kindness

(The Servant)

I love my wife. There are many who boast of the most supportive spouse, but they are mistaken. No one compares to my missus. She does not complain or nag, despite the many reasons I offer her daily. She cares and loves me for who I am, not who this world would make me. She carefully listens to my rants and makes me tea when I'm cold. Her very definition of paradise is ten minutes of uninterrupted cuddles. She will go to nearly any length for a friend and never think twice. She is always willing, always there, and always kind. Need help? She will give it. Need someone to listen

to and a shoulder to cry on? None is more in-
viting.

How does she do it? we wonder. How can
one person do so much? But what if all that
was only surface deep? What if you tear away
all the niceties and friendly manners? What if
got to their core, their heart? God makes nothing that isn't beautiful, but are His definition
of beauty and ours the same? Why are servants
really here? What is God showing us?

We know what we think is the truth.

They are here to serve us, duh. They make
for a positive environment. They meet our every need and do so smiling. How nice of God
to give them to us. That's the key to successful
church, family, and nation, after all. All the re-
search says so, now anyway. Positive environment is the key. If only we would strip all the
conflict and negativity and meet everyone's ba-

sic needs, the world would be better. No more crime, no more abuse, no more evil. Because, of course, man isn't really evil, it's just his environment that corrupts him. Get a couple of nice churchgoers in there and they will turn it right around. They will witness to him with their lives. Show him the love of Jesus with their actions.

One hundred years ago many men thought similar thoughts. They thought, "if only they could remove the corrupt system and replace it with a pure one. One that treats all men equal. One that meets everyone 's basic needs equally. Men under such a system would instantly turn into saints without the help of God," they thought. "Children would be raised by us all in a paradise of camaraderie." So they started to call each other comrade; they were all brothers after all, and conquered half the world with their ideas. Of course, the great communism experiment failed terribly. Millions died, nations were destroyed, and those men who should have become saints become only more beast-like.

So no, a positive environment is not the end all. It is not what God is showing us in the servant. Our comfort is not of great importance to God. Suffering is not evil. Going without is holy at times. God even has a name for a holy type of going-without: it's called fasting. And fasting stands contrary to our entire church doctrine and our idea of the servant. Because to fast is to deny oneself of his basic needs. To say, "God is enough. I don't need something else."

So if the servant does not exist to meet our needs, to help us, what do they do? What is God showing us in this masterpiece? In a word: Submission. They exist to show us how to give God glory. They show us how the economy of the Kingdom of Heaven works. They are the loving kindness of God made flesh and bone. They are his benevolence. But not so we may have someone to help our new, probably-won't-last boyfriend move into his new place. No, they are here to teach us how to submit to God, then give glory back for the blessing He pours out from our submission.

That is, put simply, why everything exists: to give God glory by submitting under His rule (Isaiah 48:9-11, Isaiah 43:6-7, Isaiah 43:25, Psalm 25:11, l Corinthians 10:31).

But wait, God isn't selfish like that, is he? He gave everything for me in return for... nothing, right? Yeah, that is what I learned since Sunday school. Christ died for me. God loved us so much He sent his only son so we could live, that's in the bible too, isn't it? I mean, if I was the only person on earth, Christ would still have died just for me. He loves me that much, right?

Wait a minute; if that was true, why didn't Christ come down and save Adam and Eve after they sinned? Wasn't time yet, you say? Agreed, but if His goal was to save us because of His great love for us then it should have been. So I guess there is something more to it all. Something deeper.

So what was Christ doing when He blessed all those people? What was the point of all those healings? Why did He go to the cross? To take away sin, yes, but why would the Son of God care? Have we ever considered that? Have we ever stepped out of our collective selfishness long enough to wonder why Christ, son of the Living God, would bother? David did when he wrote, "Who is man that you take notice of him?" (Psalm 8:4).

Well it was out of love, you say. Sure it was,

but love for whom? That is the question. John 13, 14, and 17 all say it was not out of love of man, but love of God. Christ blessed because Father told Him to. Christ submitted to His Father to bring glory to God. For Christ Himself said He only does what His Father tells Him to (John 5:19). But wait. Christ is God, is He not? So Christ glorified himself?

How selfish. We respond in kneejerk foolishness. Self-glory? Oh dear. How ungodly.

The teachers of the day agreed. They shivered at this carpenter saying all Glory would rest on Him. They shook their heads at His blunt claims of divinity and His lack of regard for good religious custom and accepted teaching. So what, we wonder, all God does is for his own glory? That is what is written.

Confused yet?

If you are the very source of good, and the only thing worthy of glory, it would literally be sin for you not to glorify yourself. We receive His blessings so quick and lightly and don't even say thanks to the only being that deserves it.

When filled with His Spirit, servants show us that God is not interested in our superficial needs and wants. No, He is interested in what we really need. We need to be submitted to Him. He wants to bless us, but how can He bless what is at war and rebellion to Him? Have you considered that? What makes you think you can be rebel and a Christian? How can you disobey the king and know His favor? He wants to show us what truly represents a full life. He doesn't just clothe and feed us. He births us anew.

We don't need more food, more money, more cars. We need the presence of the Almighty God of the Universe. We don't need that new job; we need faith that only comes from trust. We don't need a new definition of Christianity; we need a new demonstration of Christianity.

So in the servant we find the blessing aspect of God. They take us by the hand and list out our wants and needs. Then they go through it with a pen marking each one off and replacing it with submit.

In the servant God is saying, "This is the true blessing. Not receiving gifts or help, but submitting. That is what it means when I show loving kindness. Stop looking for earthy treasures. Submit to Me and you store up heavenly treasures. That is what it is to be blessed. To be rewarded. To be rich."

Perspective

(The Teacher)

He is wearing glasses. I suppose he has to with his nose always in a book. He seems a bit nerdy, sure, but he hardly has a ranger costume under his to-scale Enterprise model. No, he is a notch or two down from that. Brainy, but doesn't rub your face in it. Pleasant enough to be around, and not afraid to admit when he is wrong.

His knowledge is as broad-based as it gets. Ask him any question on any subject and he will have something to say, or will want to discover more about it. And what he has to say tends to sound right enough to us anyway.

And he isn't cocky about it. Not cocky like others are, he just knows what he knows and is more than able to back it up with convincing facts and studies. He dances with words like others do gals. He seems to really know how it all fits together. His curiosity is endless. He seems driven mad by a quest he can't explain. For with every fact, every theory and every conclusion, he draws from them that he is closer to finishing his masterpiece.

It is a colossal product no one can see or touch, or even grasp. For his structures are not built with steel beams but with dates, times, and documents. And it is no skyscraper he is constructing but the universe itself, for he is desperate to know... everything. He wants to see how a butterfly's wing can redirect storms. He must grasp why the speed of light is that number and not this one. Why are our eyes made to see light and not sounds? How does that change who we are and how we think? And what is light anyway? Why can light exist apart from its source? What is dark? Does shadow have dimensions? Can nothing have mass?

He must know, not so he can impress us. We wouldn't know what he is talking about anyway. No, he must gather it all up so he can form an image, a system, of how it all works. He wants to see the big picture and how the millions of small pictures fit into it all to make it up. Like a giant puzzle of constantly changing pieces. He needs to see it. How the river flows, the tree grows, and the cattle roam. Because until all his questions are answered, he won't know if he is living right.

And that is what terrifies our beloved teacher. That if he steps in the wrong place, he will start a chain reaction that he can't control or hope to stop. And this chain reaction could lead to destruction on a scale beyond his current calculations and possible imagining! So he studies. He studies everything and how everything affects everything else.

He must see where the pieces fit.

No wonder they can seem distant, distracted and indecisive to us narrow-minded. You ask one on a date and she doesn't think whether it would be a good time or not. She isn't even considering the fact you are offering her free food. No, she is instantly weighing all the possibilities against one other.

What if he doesn't like me and I like him? I'll be heartbroken then I'll start eating too much again to comfort myself, and before I know it I will be struggling with my weight just like my mother does and will die of a heart attack alone, living as a fat shut-in.

Or, what if he likes me and I can't see it going anywhere so he, being crushed, runs out to the closest slut he can find and proposes marriage on the spot. Then after a shotgun wedding, they move into a trailer and have a dozen kids but she, being a slut at heart, cheats on him, takes what little he has in divorce court and doesn't even let him see his kids. Then he, falling into utter depression, kills himself.

Nope, better play it safe.

"I'm busy that night, so sorry."

So what to do with these silly social outcasts? We could lock them up! No, they figured out how to use light to broadcast our favorite television program right to our laptops. Better to keep them around but out of the way. Let them debate endlessly with each other on whether viruses are alive or not. We have better things to do. Because who cares how it all works anyhow? We just know it does. What could God want us to see in them?

Certainly not how my decisions have consequences. No, Christ just loves me anyway. We don't live under the old law anymore. What use is a man who God gives universal perspective to, anyhow?

Sure, it would have saved us some headache if we had listened when warned about the direct connection between free love and STDs, but we got rubbers for safety now. And maybe, just maybe, things would be better if someone had told us that fathers really are important in a child's development, and that giving a kid everything they want and never punishing the brat makes for ruinous adults. And I suppose a friendly warning about how sickness is as much a spiritual issue as it is a physical would have been nice. But we know better. Trial and error is the modern way, after all.

So what has God to show us in the teacher? He shows us covenant. They are God's perspective. They see the macro and the micro simultaneously. The project he is working on, whether he knows it or not, is seeing God's covenant with man. Because once you have covenant, everything falls into place.

He makes it all fit. He shows me why Christ had to be born of a virgin, because of covenant. He shows me why I no longer cut sheep's throats open, because of covenant. He shows me why dumping myself in water is not enough, because of covenant.

He takes away our excuses. For with a teacher running around no one can claim they didn't know. (Didn't care to know and didn't ask is much more like it.) They see how much effect a change in church bylaws will have in fifty years. They know the paths we drift down. They see the pits at the end of them. They see where sin comes in and how it will destroy us.

They are the part of God that says, "Break covenant with me and you form covenant with Satan. Nothing you do is outside the authority of your covering. You only do what your covering allows. So keep covenant with Me and I will make you Princes and High Priests (royal priesthood, yes?)."

For, through covenant, Christ was given all authority over heaven and earth and then, because of that covenant, we can disciple nations (notice it doesn't say men or people. No, no, no. We are to disciple nations. Matthew 28:18-19).

Mirror

(The Exhorter)

He has been your pastor for twenty years. He has pastored the church for forty. You know him well. You tell him all your secrets and share with him all your fears. You trust him or, at least, you thought you did. It's all that new worship leader's fault anyway. Changing up the music like he did. It was fine the way it was before, thank you very much. But now it is all falling apart. This deacon thinks this. That elder said that. The small groups debate endlessly on it.

"Why does it have to be so loud?" that is all you wonder. "New world. Gotta reach the kids, sure. But do we have to damage their hearing in the process?"

And then there is the calm in the storm: the pastor. No matter who he talks to, he puts them at ease. He agrees with everybody while not disagreeing with anybody. He made you feel like it is all gonna be OK.

And yet, you know it isn't.

The more you watch the master peacekeeper at work, the more uneasy you feel around him. I mean, how can a man talk to two opposing sides and have both leave the meeting thinking he agreed with them? There is something sinister in how genuine he looks as he shakes your hand, listens to your complaints, and says he understands. There is something false in his milky grey positions on controversial issues. He has mastered the art of saying nothing in five hundred words or more. You can't explain why he makes you uneasy, you love the man. You don't even know it, you only feel it.

It is like his face is not a face at all, but instead is a mirror. It shines your own face right back at you. Saying, "I know you, I am you. I understand you. We are basically the same." And as long as the mirror is facing you, you agree and even feel warm in its glow.

But as soon as it turns away, you are left as cold as when you came. So you come back for more, everyone does. Circles of people beg for time in front of the mirror. They all want to feel its comforting glow. They say things like, "What a great counselor he is," or "He just comforts me and makes me truly believe God has got a plan for me. I feel better after talking to him, of course nothing has really changed, but I feel better." But then it strikes you. What is behind the mirror?

What if the answer is nothing?

Would it unsettle you to find a person, so full of life, was empty of personality? And what if God made him that way on purpose? Would you scratch your head? Doesn't someone have to have a personality of their own to be called a person? How horrid of God to not make someone a full individual. But Christ's bride isn't an individual, is she? No, He wants to marry the whole church, doesn't he? That's what Ephesians says. It makes sense, we suppose. No single soul is great enough to be called His bride. It would take all of us as a pure community to be equal to the task. So what aspect of God is He showing in these mirror-faced people?

Romans 1.

God will make himself known. It is His promise to us. But of course we think of angels and swirling lights when we think of God

revealing himself. It is all about the 'ah-ha moment' and the gooey feeling we get during that
one song. That's what that means, right? Or
maybe He is supposed to give us dreams and
visions. He did it for Joseph, why not me?

Plus, you can't say that a pastor who just
makes everyone feel good is showing me God,
can you? Well, a mirror shows what it is pointed at, and no matter how off target they are,
they are still mirrors. So if your darling, old
pastor is pointed at you, he reflects you and
you take comfort in that. He assures you with
your own voice. "You aren't that bad" he says,
"God loves you anyway. He knows you try.
Christ fulfilled the old law anyway. So when
Christ said be perfect as God is perfect (Matthew 5:48) he meant something else. I think if
you take it to the Greek it makes more sense. It
fits with what you want to hear anyhow. What
do all those scholars who wrote the translation

know anyway? I'm sure the gay kid with a blog knows better."

But what if?

What if something radical happened?

What if he became pointed, not at you, but at God? And what if he stayed pointed at God? He would actually... you know... reflect God. Then he might start acting like Jesus, and no one wants that- with His constant challenging and lack of compromise.

America is built on compromise, darn it. Not everyone can have their way. I mean sure, Christ comforts and heals us, but then he has the nerve to say, "sin no more."

"That's not possible," we reply. "Exactly," Christ says back. "That's why you need me. Because without me, you keep right on sinning. It's your nature. Here look. But come to me and I will give you my Father's nature, now look at that. Then you won't only stop sinning, you will forget how to sin."

And that is what the exhorter does. He shows us the face of God. Then he shows me my face again. And when I see the face of God compared to my own, I know I am lacking. But then the mirror smiles and says, "Don't worry. God has a plan for you. He wants to conform your face into His. Doesn't that sound marvelous?" Then he shines God's light on me again which is a warmth that doesn't fade once the mirror turns away. After that the exhorter can teach me what it is to worship, because until I see the face of God, I won't have a clue.

Intimacy

(The Nurturer)

Everybody loves a wedding. Dashing color, brilliant music, and the food-oh the food. Two people joined in holy union promising to love each other until the end of time. There is really only one problem: no one has a clue what it means to love like that.

Yeah, the groom loves her, but let's be reasonable here, he loves pizza and football too. And she wants to be a good wife but submit? What is this, the eighteen-hundreds? She had career goals, and he should just adapt according. But they love each other.

Do we even know what that blasted word

means? Do we get love? Sure, we sing a lot about it, and like to go to movies dedicated to the issue. I have written more than a few sappy love poems myself, thank you very much. But what is love? Real love. Not the love that ends as soon as cock meets kitty. No, the deeper kind. The kind that transcends our relation-ships. The kind the universe bends to because it is so powerful. The kind those love songs tried to tell us about.

We don't know that love. We want to, but we don't.

We taste it when we are young. Before the realities of... well, reality sets in. That rush of desire that longs for their unbroken attention. The world is against you, and yet you just know it will be OK. As long as you have that glow in their eyes and yours that makes the whole room as comfortable as a fluffy, broken-in couch.

Puppy love.

Young Love.

Sure, it's cute. It makes a great story for sinking ships, but we live in the real world.

But maybe there is something to those foolish teenage flings. Maybe they show us we have lost something in our increasing years. But what is it? It isn't sex. Nope, still want plenty of that. It isn't even our wish to see our better halves. Maybe not all the time, mind you, but we just get used to them being there.

So what is it?

What did we lose?

What did we lose?

Then it hits us like a hammer. We will be at some party, some get-together, and some old friend will drop an embarrassing story about your college years in your unsuspecting wife's lap. And she will look at you puzzled and say, "You never told me that,"

We shrug it off as a slip of the memory, "Was going to get around to it, dear." But we know better. She didn't know because we didn't want her to. It hurts the image we created from the first date onwards. It destroyed the illusion we formed. And like all great magic tricks, they lose their allure once the secret is found out.

And there it is. Like a crack on the windshield staring us in the face. We don't open up to them. We aren't even that honest. Not on the things that matter anyway. Why would we be? This world taught us long ago to trust no one.

Not with the real stuff.

Not with the risky stuff.

We trust our spouse with our homes, money and children (most of us). But we will keep our feelings to ourselves, thank you. Because that's what reasonable people do: they hide. They don't want to get hurt. Cars and fortunes can be replaced, but a heart can never be unbroken.

We can't risk being seen as weak. We can't afford to let the people at church see us get angry or tired. We don't want our parents to know we don't appreciate their visits anymore. We can't be honest enough to tell our spouse how much their jokes hurt. We don't want to be exposed, naked, and let in the cold.

So we lack the one thing we claim we want most: intimacy. We have sports pals, and girl's night out, and bible studies for the religious, bless them. But who are we kidding? People terrify us. We can't let them in. They might break something, or take something. No, we have to hide who we really are under layers of humor, and pride, and some self-righteousness for good measure. Because to just be ourselves would carry risk, and those that desire intimacy enough to risk it are braver than we.

And they are.

Compelled by love to seek openness. Openness with themselves. Openness with people. And most importantly, openness with God. So they risk. They brave the cold coil of rejection's harsh glare. They become hurt beyond measure, pick up the pieces and say, "God, I will trust... one more time."

Of course it isn't like they have a choice, is it? Those who are the embodiment of God's intimacy, they don't see people. They see living books walking around. And all they want to do is let you crack open the pages of their inner being and to let them do the same to you.

Come on, read a little. Here are some good pages for you. I want you to see them. I don't show them to many. Can I see your favorite part now? Can I read your inner pose?

But unlike a book, there is no closing chapter. Intimacy does not cease when the last fact is known. Dare I say that is when it begins! It is the fine wine, growing in value over time. It is the wedding feast where our Lord brought out the best for last, and even better after. And we say, "I thought we were close before, but that was only a shadow of the relationship we have now. And this is only a shadow of the closeness we will have in the future."

They want that. They want to be a part of your life and have you be a part of theirs. And in the process teach us something we have forgotten.

How to be intimate.

How to be intimate with other people but also to be intimate with God. To be completely vulnerable with our Father. Letting our walls down for all who ask. This is what God is showing us in the nurturer. He is saying, "You must remember. How can you be joined together as a church and live as separate castles? How can you be a part of me and not be intimate with me?"

We know we are not intimate with God. It is proven every time we force out another dreadfully formalized prayer. Really, when was the last time we called up our dad and said, "Dear Earthly Father?" But we can't conceive what it is to be intimate with God who we can't see because we can't grasp what it is to be open with people who we can see.

And that is why we need the nurturers. To show us the way. To show us how. To take us by the hand and teach us to be open again. To teach us to abandon the comfort of polite lies and be ourselves. Then, and only then, they can do their truest calling. They can teach us to pray.

Creation

(The Leader)

Humility conquers pride.

This is what the artist Caravaggio etched into David's sword of his last painting, "David with the Head of Goliath." It's a self-portrait. But unlike what you would expect, the painter doesn't make himself the young victorious David. No, it is the severed head of the evil giant that holds his resemblance.

Why?

Well it comes to what is on the sword, "Humility conquers pride." It was a lesson Caravaggio never learned in his life. He instead lived a brutal life of street fights, drunken antics, and small insults with big repercussions. Even as he painted masterpiece after masterpiece and showed complete control over his brush, he never could control himself.

We all know one: the tortured genius. Full of himself and full of ideas. He has vision. He knows it all. He has it all figured it. He can out-talk the best of them. He dominates his circle of friends. He out-geeks the geeks, out-jocks the jocks and out-rednecks the hillbillies. He is the top of the mountain in his domain and rarely ventures from it.

"What makes him the expert?" some ask, "At what school did he receive his degree?" The only one that matters: himself.

So yeah, he is pompous, but don't try to tell him that. He won't get it. He isn't pompous, he thinks, he is right! But what if he is? Worse yet, what if he isn't in the flesh like we would automatically assume. What if he happens to be in the spirit? What if our definition of arrogant isn't the same as God's? What if he has a plan?

Yeah, but who does he think he is- bossing me around? He doesn't even have a degree; I have three! He won't seek advice like our old pastor did, and compromise? Bah! Forget about it.

So where does that brash, calm and complete certainty come from? Know it wasn't from his grades. He did well when he wanted to, I heard. But he hardly ever turned in the homework, lazy bum.

And then there is his passion for it all. It only makes the cockiness worse. He caught some kid teasing a neighborhood boy. He didn't have any of that. He tore the kid up one side and down the other. He could have cared less what the bully's parents had to say. He doesn't seem Godly to me, all that yelling, but Christ yelled, didn't he? And little king David didn't care much for bullies either, huh?

So when we talk of leaders we really are talking about creators. Some create art like poor old Caravaggio. But God, the master creator, isn't going to be limited by a single medium, no. He will branch out past our ability to comprehend. And those made in the aspect of God's creativeness will do so too.

They live to create, to build, to make. They don't much care what it is as long as it has never existed before. I mean, what really is the difference between creating a scene with paint and creating a new industry? They form and compose and bring order to whatever they touch. Doesn't being able to create draw you closer to being in the image of God? Can you be in the image of a creating God and not create?

Don't like it?

Very good, go away.

They don't need you, anyway.

They are creating new worlds here. Bringing to life visions no one has ever had, and you want to get between the sculpture's chisel and the stone? He knows what he wants. He sees it clear as day and feels no need to share his vision with you.

Doesn't sound like the God you read about you say?

You are right.

It doesn't.

It sounds like the God of Job though. Truly, how hard could it have been to explain things to poor Job? "Satan made a bet that you would break, and you didn't. Good job buddy." But no, God did no such thing. Why? The leader understands why.

Because God was in control, and if you cannot trust that, go away. I don't need your doubts. I have worlds to build. Do they seem arrogant? Anyone who is sure they are right seems arrogant. That is not the right question. The question is, "Are they spirit-filled?" For if they are the God kind of right then I want to be arrogant too. If they have the vision of God, sign me up. If they are building His kingdom, I'll go there with a song and a cheer.

If not, there is an etched sword waiting for them.

But those in the spirit have God's vision in mind. He is creating not what man desires but what Almighty God longs to see. And those leaders aren't interested in your opinion of them or if they rub you the wrong way. They have directives from the God Most High. They have worlds to create. And in the process, they teach us what it is to have vision. For without vision, we will die (Proverbs 29:18).

Revelation

(The Mercy)

Mommy's yelling again. Something about the dishwasher ruining her soothing hot shower she was been waiting all day for. And how it proves my father is as insensitive as she thinks. Dad stands like a marble statue refusing to let her get a rise out of him. But of course, tragically, that is really all she wants and needs.

The more he tries to understand what she is so upset about, the more upset she gets. Because she doesn't want him to understand, she doesn't understand herself. It isn't even about understanding. It is about feeling. She wants him to feel exactly what she is feeling, and he just doesn't get it.

Well, how could he? In this world of careful academic study, emotions have lost much of their voice. We have replaced them with ritual instead.

Why express my anger when that could land me in anger management. No, play it nice. Smile. Shake their hand. I'll let my anger out on their reputation later behind their back. That is a much healthier approach.

Instead of allowing ourselves to be overwhelmed with grief of a loved one's death, we sit in the funeral with a stoic face. Then to show how much we hurt, we let a few whimpers slip. Saying, "See, look at me people. My love for the departed was so great it pushes the limits of my control. No need to worry though, I tucked it back away quickly."

No, why have to deal with your anxiety that announces your lack of trust in God when you can just take a pill.

It's alright. Everyone struggles from time to time. I'm just in a hard spot. The medication is just helping me deal with it. I have a condition. The doctor told me so. Perfectly safe, he said. The pill makers told him so on the golf course.

We learn it from when we are young: how to control our emotions. And that isn't a bad thing, but geez; can't we control emotion without killing it? Doctors of all schools of thought and science try to shove them in their intellectual boxes, but somehow they just won't fit. Sure, we get the evolutionary need for fear and even enjoyment. It makes sense an ape man would need enjoyment to know what is good for him and what is bad, and fear to flee what will hurt him. But sadly the world isn't that simple. For mixed in with these staples of survival are things like guilt, shame, regret, envy, grief, and love. What is the evolutionary advantage of grief? Why should I care if my parents die, ripe in their old age?

We come up with hollow answers and push them aside, but the truth nags at us. For as much as we have tried to banish shame from our lives, it continues to plague us. We use drugs to dull our minds, to reserve ourselves, and to make life more manageable, but these at-best only act as rose-colored glasses. Once removed, the scene has not changed. The reality is still the same, and our emotions are as real as ever. They tear at us. Gnaw on us. We banish them as we can, and yet we still have them.

And then when we try to select emotions for deletion, we find that God, in a cruel prank of love, has bundled them all together. In the act of removing regret we lose joy. When we cut away shame we also strip off peace. And when we dig into guilt we lose our compassion. They are all tied together and all made for His glory. To be used for His purpose, and to reveal to us His nature.

So how do we navigate through this sea of emotions? How do we know how to show sorrow without resorting to a cheap mask? Is it possible to be a Christian and not have emotions? Is it possible to be intimate and not be genuine in showing them?

No.

Emotions are raw, real things. God gave them to use and even sent instruction manuals. The mercy person says, "Look. This is what this emotion looks like. You have forgotten. You have spent so long being numb; you don't remember what joy looks like. You have lost what it is to mourn. You have abandoned your natural spring. Remember now. This is what feelings are and how to use them to the glory of God rather than your own ends."

And then they show us what feelings do. They show us how God feels. They show us how God feels about us, about this world, and about our lives. They show us how we hurt Him when we rebel against Him. They show us how He grieves at sin. They show us how He rejoices in what He made.

But we don't want that.

It all sounds too messy.

Someone might think I'm weird, or too spiritual. Besides, God isn't like that. God doesn't feel. He is distant, impersonal. Or at least He has always been in my life. I'm not comfortable with a God that feels. It brings Him far too close to earth, much closer than we want Him. Then

He might see my life, and what I am doing with it. Or worse yet, I might discover He doesn't feel the same about things that I do. I might find out He isn't so gun-ho about my ministry as I think He should be. That He doesn't care much for our church's mission trip, or doesn't care much for our church.

It terrifies us to have a God so real. We can't ritualize such a God. We can't put Him in our box. We might find out He hates us and all we are doing. We might find out He is not as impressed with our nation as we think He should be.

And then to be able to feel His feelings, well... that just won't do. We don't want to feel the disappointment in our gut. We don't want to know his mournful pain. 'Cause then we might lose sight of our pitiful problems, and we can't have that, can we? No, we certainly can't have our sin hurt, or our foolishness shame us, or our rebellion cause us guilt.

No sir, God can stay in His old book where He belongs. We are just fine with our prescription narcotics, thank you very much. We don't need to feel God's emotions, so He can just take those designed in that aspect of Him back. We will be a body without a heart. We will be a church without a soul. We are just fine.

But we are not fine! We are so turned over in our problems we can't see the one thing Christ should give us: hope. Does the world suck? Yes, it does. But God says He has overcome the world. Is it painful? Yes! But God says he will give rest to the burdened and peace to the troubled.

And that is what the mercy person reveals. They show us the hope and the cheer. They don't sugarcoat our troubles. That would be deceitful. Honey on the offering. No, they say,

"You're right. It sucks, but the joy of the Lord is my strength, and if you hold to God, He will save you." Not because you deserve it. Not because you talked your way into it. Not because 'He just loves you so much.' But because it is written!

God, in His infinite strangeness, has placed His revelation not in the knowledge of the teacher, or the power of the prophet, or the hands of the servant, or the heart of the nurturer, or the smile of the exhorter, nor even the strength of the leader. No, He placed the revelation of His goodness into the joyous cries of the spirit-filled mercy. Who say with the emotions of the GodHead Himself burning on their tongues, "I am with you always, even to the very end of the age." (Matthew 28:20).

For in that state, the mercy person can show me true mercy. He teaches me how to praise God in all things, not just what I am comfort-

What Wonder is This?

(Conclusions)

Four years ago, a madman told me God said I was wonderful. The statement disturbed me. But what unsettled me more was that the statement disturbed me.

It is true, of course.

I am wonderful.

I am the creation of God and made in his image. I have no choice but to be wonderful. I can't help it in spite of myself. So who does God say I am?

His.

Made by Him, from Him, for Him.

I regret to confess I may have tricked you. You may have thought this book was about you, about us as humans. Nothing is further from the truth. This little work is about Him. For when He formed you and me in our mothers' wombs, He did not create something entirely new. He simply took a bit of Himself and put it there. And when all these little bits of Him come together for His glory, we begin to be woven and tied into one body- into one being. Then on our glorious wedding day, we, the church of individuals melted into one body, will be presented to Christ as the perfect bride. A bride of the same kind and same species as our husband. Less than Him, but of His essence.

For Adam may have had a dog for a friend and a cat for a roommate, but God made something from him, like him, for him as a wife.

Which is why Adam said upon seeing Eve for the first time, "Flesh of my flesh and bone of my bone." (Genesis 2:23).

You may feel blessed after hearing these things. You may feel that you are closer to God, that you see it now. You may wish to thank me. Don't. I have done you no great favor today. I have heaped condemnation on you, in fact. For you cannot unsee what you have seen. You cannot unhear what you have heard. I have showed you who God made you to be. I have showed you what He excepts you to give to His church. You now have no excuse. You cannot claim ignorance anymore. You know the good you ought to do.

The Prophet is teach us to see the unseen. The Servant is to teach us to submit. The Teacher is to teach us God's covenant. The Exhorter is to teach us how to worship God. The Nurturer is to teach us to pray. The Leader is to show us vision. The Mercy is teach us how to be thankful in all things with praise. Now, if you choose to not give what God has given you to give His church, you walk through the blood of Christ as an unholy thing and there is no sacrifice left for you. (Hebrews 10:29)

If God spoke to you.

If the Kingdom is nearer.

If you have sought and not yet found.

If.

www.godsplacewichita.com

www.ingramcontent.com/pod-product-compliance
Lightning Source LLC
Chambersburg PA
CBHW020602030426
42337CB00013B/1167

* 9 780615 930404 *